South West Africa

1   The brick-red dunes at Sossus Vley

South West Africa
and its indigenous peoples

by
Alice Mertens

with an introduction by
Stuart Cloete

Taplinger Publishing Co., Inc., New York

First published in the United States, 1967
TAPLINGER PUBLISHING CO. INC.
29 East Tenth Street
New York, New York 10003

This book is dedicated to Dr. and Mrs. Markus Zschocke. Especially to Markus, who with his tremendous knowledge of the northern Native Territories in South West Africa, which he has administered for 17 years as Chief Veterinary Officer, has been of invaluable help to me. I also want to thank the missionaries, cattle inspectors, government officials and the Cape Town Museum, without whose assistance this book would not have been possible.

Library of Congress Catalog Card Number: 67-12482

Produced by Zokeisha Publications Ltd.
9, Azabu-Roppongi Minato-ku, Tokyo
Printed in Japan, Bound in Scotland

Contents

COLOUR ILLUSTRATIONS

*All the photographs in this book are by Alice Mertens
except for the following: 47, 48: Mr. C. Richards,
Cape Town; 89: Photo Allers, Walvis Bay*

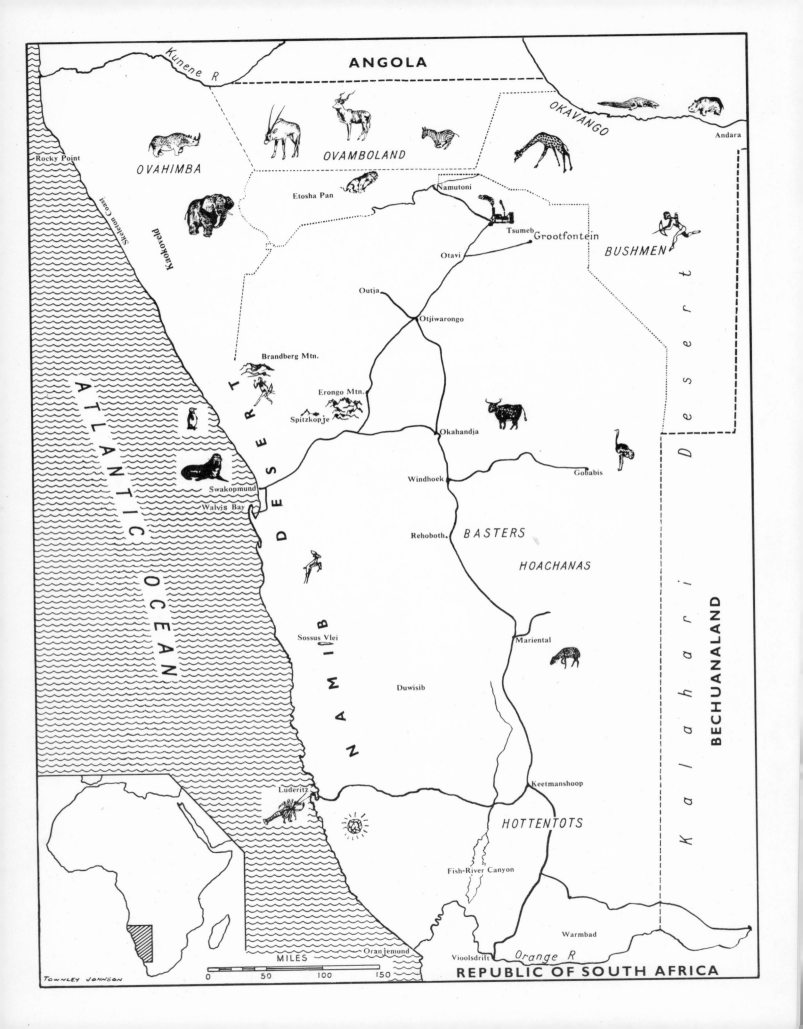

Introduction by Stuart Cloete

SOUTH WEST AFRICA, a vast, arid, semi-desert bounded by the Republic of South Africa, the Bechuanaland Protectorate, Angola and the Atlantic Ocean, is in the news to-day. It is a subject of dispute in the United Nations, who claim that South Africa has no right to exercise the mandate over the territory given to the Republic—then the Union of South Africa—by the defunct League of Nations after World War I. The outcome of this dispute is still in doubt.

Like all Africa south of the Sahara, South West has no history. The Damaras and Bushmen and Hottentots seem to have been there since time began. The Ovambos and Hereros drifted in from the north. The Ooorlams and Basters (mixed Hottentots and white) came up from the south.

All these races lived separately, divided by vast distances of nothingness, pinned by the scarcity of water to their own areas. Migrating, fighting when forced by population pressure on their meagre resources, they impinged one on the other.

The Ovambo were chiefly agriculturists, the Hereros a pastoral people with great herds of cattle, and the Hottentots with great herds of goats. The Ooorlams, mounted and armed with guns, were the real masters of the land till the Germans came.

The first white man known to have visited this barren coast was Diego Câo, a Portuguese Captain. He put up a stone cross (at Cape Cross) and hoisted a Portuguese flag, taking it in the name of Jesus and King Henry, and sailed away. This was in 1484. Two years later Diaz landed at Angra Pequena in 1486, now Luederitz Bay, frightened the sea birds—its only inhabitants—and also sailed away. There was nothing here and the sands knew no white man's spoor till the seventeenth and eighteenth centuries, when some explorers came and also left, having lost their draft oxen, suffered much hardship and only gained in experience.

A few whalers hunted these leviathans from Walvis (Whale) Bay. Visitors only, who came to kill and fry out their blubber in the pots they set up in the sand, they had no lack of fuel from the wreckage that had been washed up for centuries. But at last, in the second half of the eighteenth century, Europeans crossed the Orange. Jacob Coetzee reached Warmbad. Hendrik Hop got as far as Keetmanshoop. Willem van Reenen reached Modderfontein. And after 1800 some Ooorlams, Hottentots mounted and armed, settled amongst the Hottentots of Great Namaland at Bethanie, Gobabis, Windhoek and Gibeon. In 1805 the first mission station was established at Warmbad and destroyed six years later. Missionary Schmelen then built the now oldest mission station at Bethanie.

Meanwhile, the whole country was in an uproar, with everyone fighting everyone else. The Hereros, who had displaced the Bechuanas in the Okahandja district, were conquered by Jonker Afrikaner, the Napoleon of South West Africa, the famous Ooorlam leader, a one-eyed bandit. In 1850 Jonker Afrikaner destroyed the mission at Okahandja, and drove the Hereros into the wilderness where he raided them for years. In 1870 the so-called ten-year peace between the Hereros and Hottentots began.

By 1870 a hundred and fifty Europeans had settled in South West Africa and the Basters from the Cape Province had arrived at Rehoboth.

Although the territory is so immense and lightly populated, almost empty in fact, the native wars and raids continued, were even inherent due to the sparsity of grazing and the shortage of water—disputes common to all desert countries.

But Africa was now being carved up like a joint of mutton. England, France, and Belgium sliced themselves big chunks of it. Only Germany was out—left with the leavings. She had her eye on South West but England, who wanted no part of it, declared Walvis Bay, the only good harbour, a British possession in 1878, painted it red on the map, and in 1880 sent a magistrate to hoist the Union Jack. As a kind of patriotic counter a German merchant Adolph Luederitz all on his own, acquired the Bay of Angra Pequena from a Hottentot chief, and at last, in 1884, succeeded in selling the idea of a German colony to Bismarck. The German Reich now made treaties with everyone in sight, and German South West Africa was born, a status symbol rather than a profitable concern, with a British enclave around the only good anchorage.

Some Boers came in, welcomed as colonists by the Germans. More Germans arrived. What their feeling must have been when they approached this desolate coast is not difficult to imagine. In 1896 local tribal differences were put down. There were a number of revolts in Africa at the end of the nineteenth century—the Matabele in Rhodesia, the Shangaans in Mozambique—all fruitless. Time had caught up with the Africans at last, as it had with the American Indians and the Australian aborigines.

After they had settled down at Windhoek in 1890, with their usual industry the Germans set to work to try to make half a blade of grass grow where none had grown before. They built villages that grew slowly into towns, built railroads—narrow gauge it is true, but they carried men and goods. They explored. They developed.

But in 1897 all Africa had a setback—the rinderpest, which killed hundreds of thousands of cattle and probably millions of head of game. It spread its net from the Indian Ocean to the Atlantic, and reached down from the Sudan into the Cape Colony. Never had the vultures feasted so well.

But the course of Colonial development was now set. Beginning a hundred odd years ago it has now run its course. It only remains to be seen if the African can pick up the burden that the white man has put down.

In 1901 the great copper mine at Tsumeb began work. In 1903 the

Bondelswarts revolted; in 1904 the Hereros revolted, and massacred 123 Europeans. They were defeated and driven into the Kalahari. The Ovambos, taking advantage of the trouble, attacked the fort at Namutoni. Then the Hottentots revolted and were put down.

Tribal war is an African behaviour pattern, a product of greed, land hunger and the young men's boredom. Forays for cattle and women, as tests of manhood, were endemic among most tribes.

In 1908 the first diamonds were discovered near Luderitzbucht.

In 1914 the first World War came to South West as South African troops under Louis Botha landed there. In July, 1915, the Germans surrendered.

In 1919 Germany lost South West and her other African colonies as a result of the Treaty of Versailles. In 1920 the League of Nations entrusted the country to the Union of South Africa as a C-Mandate (Art. 22) to be administered as an integral part of the Union. (Now the Republic of South Africa.) To-day the legality of the Mandate is being questioned by the United Nations Organization.

That in a nutshell is the history of this vast territory, that covers an area of 822, 907 square kilometres with a total population of half a million, distributed as follows (1960):

European	73,154
Ovambo	241,123
Okavango and Caprivi Tribes	42,593
Ovahimba	12,381
Herero	35,635
Bushman	14,547
Damara	43,602
Nama	32,417
Cape Coloured	23,983
Others	5,629

It is somewhat difficult to see how so empty a land can be a threat to world peace, as is claimed by the Afro-Asians. But South West remains an enchanted land, producing astonishing riches out of the sea, its deserts, and savannahs: diamonds, copper, lead, tin, manganese, fluorspar, beryllium, cadmium, caesium, germanium, vanadium, lithium, phosphates, kyanite, columbite, salt, semi-precious stones, cattle, karakul sheep, woolled sheep, karakul skins and wool hides, pilchards, rock lobsters, dried fish, fish meal, guano.

A curious mixture that breaks down to its main products—copper, lead, diamonds and karakul skins from the land, and pilchards and rock lobsters from the sea.

These are the big things. But it still remains difficult to explain the charm of this country to someone who has never been there. The charm of South West Africa—a lost land of bush, desert, mountain and arid veld.

It has the finest dust in the world and more of it. In some places a single karakul sheep requires 30 hectares of grazing to stay alive. Night drivers have to be careful because the kudu on the roads, dazzled by the lights, are liable to leap into the cars.

Tall Herero women, dressed in fashions of the Regency, made still taller by their folded turbans, move with reluctant dignity, dragging their brilliant skirts along the ground. They will only do laundry and needlework—this they do superbly at a snail's pace. Ovambos, Basters, Damaras, Ovahimbas, Bushmen and Hottentots, all weave in and out of a scene where a short to-day has been superimposed upon an endless yesterday. The old Africa is very near the surface in South West, and this may be the secret of the country's fascination.

It is an empty, silent land. The population, both white and black, is thinly scattered. But there is the feeling of great possibilities latent here, of riches that remain to be discovered in this Aladdin's wilderness.

Basically the culture remains German. Everyone is trilingual and there is no apparent friction between the various groups. On Saturday nights at the Continental Hotel the atmosphere is gay and European—the girls as pretty as are to be found anywhere. Their dresses come from London, Berlin, Paris or Rome. Over the open-air dance floor hangs the great African moon. Mixed with the perfume of the women is the scent of the thorns in flower and a faint odour of dust. Africa is always calling here—someone has just shot a lion that was killing stock, two more skeletons of prospectors illicitly seeking diamonds have been found among the shifting dunes; someone is just back from the Etosha Pan or the Brandberg, or is just going. Parked next to the big black Cadillac is a farmer's dusty, battered jeep.

New buildings are going up, almost as you wait, but history remains, like a backdrop to a changing scene. There will never be much industry in South West. The two prerequisites of ample labour and water are both missing, so progress will be along primary lines: the production of beef, of fruit, of fur, of guano, of salt, of fish, diamonds, copper and other minerals.

The greatest need of the territory would seem to be improved road and railway facilities, coupled with packing and refrigeration plants which would enable the products of the country to be exported via Walvis Bay to the rest of the world—and above all, water. For here, as in so much of Africa, water is the magic key. The possibilities are all there, and much more than possibility, for from here already come almost all the world's canned pilchards, almost three million karakul pelts a year; and the diamond fields of the desert and the sea are unbelievably rich.

As cattle country, much of the veld is unsurpassed, with a varying capacity of one beast to seven or ten hectares. Timber and tropical fruit can be developed in the well-watered North.

There is also a great opening for a tourist industry. There is plenty to see and to do in South West. Its highlights are, of course, the Etosha

II   An escarpment at the edge of the Namib desert

III   South West African semi-precious stones

Pan with its game and the old German fort of Namutoni that looks like something straight out of a Foreign Legion film set, the Bushman paintings of the Brandberg, the great Fish River Canyon, the Petrified Forest, the Namib Desert and the salt pans and the bird life of the Coast.

So far little has been organised to attract the visitor. The transport is poor, there are few rest houses, and not even a brochure which would tell the tourist something about the things he could see. Something like the "Tree Tops" of Kenya could be built at the Etosha Pan water holes. Some plan by which the Seal Rookery, which is unique, at Cape Cross, could be visited and photographed, could be arranged. Selected farms could be visited and gift shops selling karakul furs, wild animal skins, semi-precious stones and native curios could be organised.

Some people regard tourists as a nuisance and the industry not worth the trouble of developing, but this is a short-sighted policy. It is not merely the money spent by the tourist, there is beyond this an enormous and not immediately apparent return in the interest taken by the tourist in the territory he visits and the possibility of trade and investment growing out of what began as no more than a desire to see some strange new land. Because South West is the end of the line— on the way to Nowhere—it remains relatively unknown even to the South African Republic. Tsumeb is the end of the Southern African world. Beyond it lie Ovamboland and Angola. Beyond that Leopold-ville and the Congo. But there is no rail link between these centres.

What, then, is the charm of South West Africa? It is the paradox of the Namib Desert and the Skeleton Coast lying only one air hour away from the sophistication of Windhoek. The fact that Africa cannot be forgotten here. In the streets, mixed up with modern buildings, are ancient thorns that were here even before the Hereros came down from the North. Nor can the beauty of the light be ignored—the lilac clarity of evening in the hour that the Zulus call " the time when everything is beautiful " is something that can never be forgotten.

South West is not a pretty country. It is grand, wonderful, change-able. It has the quality of a " jolie laide ", of a woman whose individual features may not be lovely but whose variety of expression never cease to enthrall and enchant.

South West has something that no other country I have ever visited possesses. An original quality where a surprise lies in wait behind every hill. Nowhere else do the rivers run hidden under their sandy beds, beer foam more beautifully in a glass; nowhere are there prettier girls or a better chance to see something new every day. South West is still a land of opportunity for the businessman and a peephole into the past for the tourist who wants to see Africa as it used to be. The herds of game, the empty veld and the burning desert. Here peace is to be found and, in the wilder places, a silence broken only by the beating of one's own wondering heart.

South West Africa

1. This wild "mountains of the moon" country north of the Orange River produces some of the finest Persian lamb skins in the world. The karakul sheep of the semi-desert thrives on this kind of country, which may take up to 30 hectares (73 acres) to support a single sheep

2. The annual safari from Windhoek this time to the Skeleton Coast—
a barren region beyond the mountains in the background of this picture

3, *above*, Hoachanas. Established a hundred years ago, it is the oldest mission in South West Africa. Settlers from Germany followed the missionaries in the 1880's. 4, *below*, a typical sheep and cattle farm in the highlands

5, *overleaf*, the great Fish-River Canyon, near Keetmanshoop

WATER. 6, Droughts may last several years, the ground becoming
parched and cracked; 7, *right*, after heavy rain the land is transformed

WATER. 8. In a long drought thousands of cattle die. 9, *right*, after rain

10. Karakul lambs, introduced from the Buchara, are bred for their pelts. 11, *right*, a farmer's daughter with a new-born lamb

12. Duwisib, a castle built early in this century by a nostalgic German, Baron von Wolf, on the edge of the Namib Desert. On the vast Duwisib estate are bred some of the finest Karakuls in the world

13. A mountain range on the Duwisib estate, beyond which lies the Namib desert. The thorn tree in the foreground may be centuries old

14. When they can afford to, the Hereros dress with great elegance. *Above*, three school-teachers in Kaiserstrasse, the main street of Windhoek. 15, *right*, tall and graceful Herero women still dress in the style of the earliest missionary wives

With the Bushmen, the Hottentot tribes are the oldest inhabitants of South West Africa. 16, *above*, a Hottentot man, with the traditional ear-ring in his right ear to protect him from illness. 17, *right*, an old Hottentot woman

19, *above*, huts in the Warmbad Hottentot reserve. The skins and woven mats which once covered the bentwood frames have been replaced by sacks and flattened tins. 18, *left*, a Hottentot beauty. 20, *overleaf*, semi-desert country, dotted with scrub. Only karakul sheep can survive here

21-22, *left*, the distances are so great that every farmer must be his own mechanic, carpenter and mason. Wood and metal-work are therefore an important part of the curriculum in schools. 23, *above*, architectural contrast in Windhoek. Since the last war modern buildings have begun to replace those of the old German pattern

ROADS are the arteries of this land of vast distances. 24. A few are
tarred, like this one, but most have only a gravel surface. 25, *right*,
stuck in the sand of a dry river-bed. This is not unusual when one
leaves the main roads

26, *overleaf*, the annual river procession āt the Andara Roman Catholic
mission on the Okavango—one of the only three rivers of South West
Africa

28. The "Mukarob", a Hottentot word meaning "finger of God"

27, *left*, Lake Otjikoto, the crater of an extinct volcano is said to be
bottomless but is in fact connected with Lake Guinas, another lake
some twelve miles away

29-30. Two members of the Basters, who are descended from the Cape Coloureds. They migrated north from the Cape in the 1870's and are now settled around Rehoboth

31, *left*, a Koker Boom, or quiver tree. The Bushmen used the hollowed
branches to make quivers for their arrows. It can live almost without
water and is a true desert tree. 32, *above*, the *Welwitschia mirabilis*
grows on the desert coastal belt and draws all its water from the sea
fogs which roll in from the west. Its tattered leaves are yards long.
The specimen in this picture is assumed to be about 2000 years old,
from carbon tests of a smaller plant, which gave an age of 1500 years

33, *above*, the rocky landscape through which the Swakop River flows. Except after heavy rain, the river is underground, seeping through its sandy bed. 34, *right*, in this narrow canyon, which is several miles long, Zebra and other game come to water-holes protected from the sun by the rock walls. After heavy rain the passage becomes a roaring torrent

35, *overleaf*, the Kuiseb canyon at the edge of the Namib Desert, from the air

36. Kleinspitzkopje. A rocky outcrop in the Namib Desert near Usakos, an area famous for its semi-precious stones

Bushmen are a stone-age people who still survive in the Kalahari, a semi-desert region—their last remaining stronghold. When young, they have delicate heart-shaped features, like this young girl (37, *left*). When she grows older, the constant glare of the sun will affect her eyes until they become hardly more than slits. Tobacco is their greatest luxury. 38, *below*, an old woman sucking happily at her pipe made from an animal's bone

39. A Bushman hunting. The arrow's poisoned head is detachable:
the shaft falls away from it on impact, showing the hunter which spoor
to follow until the poison takes effect

40. This woman may be only 50 years old. Her cloak—the only
garment except for a loin covering—is of antelope skin

41, *above*, " Groot Spitzkopje " near Swakopmund was once a Bushman's paradise, with water and copious game. Many of their rock
paintings are found there. 42, *right*, rock paintings in South West
Africa are often found on exposed faces—some are in caves

43. Next to Spitzkopje (see picture no. 41) are the Pontok Mountains. These strangely-shaped rocks have been ground down and smoothed by the hot sand-laden desert winds which blow at all seasons of the year

IV Fort Namutoni

44. Caves in the so-called Bushman's Paradise, in the heart of the
Pontok Mountains; the walls of the lower one are covered with rock-
paintings. Until driven away by war with migrating tribes or the
depletion of the game herds on which they depended, Bushmen lived
here for hundreds of years—probably until the last century

45. The famous *White Lady* painting of the Brandberg. The age,
origin and subject of the painting—whether a " lady " or a boy—is the
subject of much speculation

46, *above*, in the Ameib cave in the Erongo mountains there is an unusual painting of a white elephant. 47, *below*, these elephants at Etosha Pan were white too, when they had dusted themselves with chalkstone sand

48, *above*, the moon rises over the Etosha Pan, which was once a great lake—and still is, for months on end, after very heavy rains. The Game Reserve around it is the largest in the world, covering 26,000 square miles, and teeming with countless game and birds. Here a flock of cranes are flying over a herd of blue wildebeest. 49, *right*, the old German fort at Namutoni on the edge of the Etosha Pan. It was built in 1907 as a defence outpost to the north, by Count Saurma-Jeltsch, on the same site as an older fort where three years before a garrison of seven German soldiers had held off an attack by 500 Ovambos for two days before escaping by night

50. Oryx at the Etosha pan. It was these buck that gave rise to the
Unicorn myth

51, *left*, Giraffe and blue wildebeest at a waterhole in Etosha Pan

52. Tsumeb, the most northerly town in South West Africa. Some seventeen different metals are mined here; Tsumeb has the biggest lead mine in Africa and the biggest copper mine south of the Limpopo

v   At Ameib in the Erongo mountains

53. Most of the labourers at Tsumeb, like this bossboy, come from the
Ovambo tribes in the north

OVAMBOLAND. 54, *above*, a girl fetching water from a dam. This country is so stoneless that the men who go south to work often bring back a stone to show the women. 55. *right*, Ukuanjama girls still use primitive methods to stamp flour from mahango, an indigenous corn

56. Women of the Ondonguenna, in the north of Ovamboland, wear
their hair in charming short pigtails

57. The Ovambo women have a passion for " jewellery ", like this
girl's belt of beads and empty cartridges

58. An Ovambo woman of the Oganjerra tribe in full regalia of carved ivory buttons and beads hanging down her back. Her bun and horns are made of palm leaf and the long false hair comes from a cow's tail

59. Humbe girl from the Angola border has used hair collected from
the whole family, interwoven with palm fibre, for this creation with
an Egyptian motif

60. *Modern Ovambos.* Christian Ovambo girls prefer to be married
in church and in European dress. The bridegroom had to buy all the
finery for both of them while he was working in the south

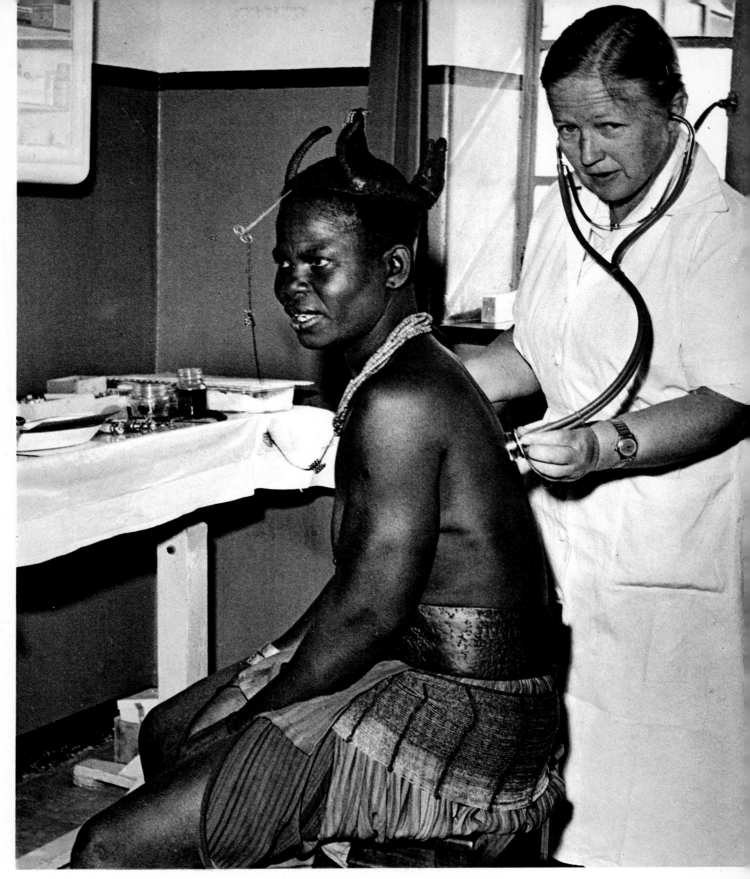

61. An Ukuanjama woman, whose hair-do is made from split cow-horns, is given a check-up in hospital. In her hair she carries a scalp-scratcher

62. A baobab by moonlight

Overleaf. 63, girls dancing an Efundula dance; 64, a woman watching
the festivities, with her child on her back. This great festival is held
every few years to mark the coming-of-age of Ovambo girls. Sustained
by the excitement and kaffir beer, the girls have to dance all night for
three nights running, while their elders watch them, feasting and drink-
ing. Few white people have ever seen this. Only after Efundula are
the girls eligible for marriage

65. Nehemia Chovalego, a rich chief of the Ukuanjama tribe with some of his eighteen wives and thirty-eight children. Since all manual work around the kraal is done by women, a rich man, who has not been converted by one of the missions, will have as many wives as he can afford, for comfort as well as prestige

66. *above*, Herero children cooking. 67. *below*, Okavango churning butter

VI Two Ovahimba women doing each others' hair, which is lengthened
with palm-fibre and smeared with ochre and fat

68. *above*, Long-horned native cattle of the Ankole type found right across Africa at this latitude. 69. *below*, Berg Damara. A woman milking goats. All natives, even on European farms, keep goats for milk and meat

As in other parts of Africa, oxen are an important means of transport. 70, *left*, a boy riding a native ox, which is guided by a string passed through the septum of the nose. 71, *above*, an ox-drawn sledge made from a tree fork. The Africans never invented a wheel, and sledges are responsible for much erosion

72. Workers for the diamond fields at Oranjemund are flown 750 miles
to and from Grootfontein. This not only saves five days' travelling
time each way but reduces diamond smuggling

73. Diamonds are the country's biggest export. To reach them whole dunes are removed, by the biggest bull-dozers in the world (*each tyre* costs £400) to uncover the gravel of the former sea-bed

74-75. To have long and straight hair is a general ambition among native women. To imitate this, Okavango women (*above* and *left*) use wild sisal, plaited rolled and smeared with fat and ochre. Ovambos use cow's tails, and Ovahimbas palm-fibre

76. Okavango mother and child

VII The Kuiseb Canyon, with the red dunes of Namib in the background

77. An Okavango woman with a wig made of wild sisal smeared with
fat and ochre

78. Mats woven from reeds, that have been flattened and dried, are used as sleeping mats, for the sides of sledges and for garden fences

79. A Chokwe craftsman from Angola making a stool. These men also
make masks for the tourist trade

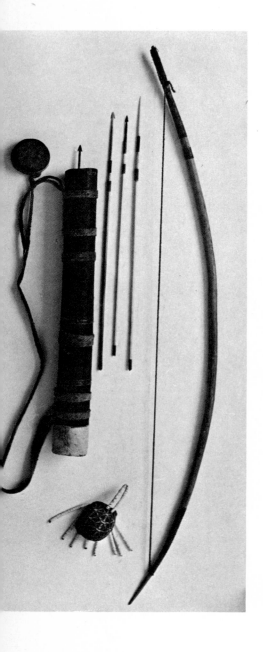

80. (a) Bushman bow-and-arrows and a tortoise shell powder box for women, (b) Okavango stool, (c) Ovambo dagger and flat baskets, (d) Ovambo storage basket, (e) Chokwe mask, (f) Okavango drum

81, *overleaf*, Ovamboland waterhole

82. Okavango men dancing while the women clap and sing

83. A big Okavango drum. Its throbbing can be heard for miles

84. Okavango girl carrying mahango cobs in a cone-shaped basket.
Baskets of this shape are found in many parts of Africa

85. Mahango corn is removed from the cob with heavy wooden pestles

86. A dugout canoe on the Okavango River

87. Okavango woman fishing with a dip trap which catches fish in the throat. The fish, dried and pounded up, are used to flavour the mahango corn porridge

88, pilchards at Walvis Bay. A great amount of the world's supply
of pilchards comes from here

89. Walvis Bay, South West Africa's only harbour, actually belongs
to the Republic of South Africa

90. *above*, Swakopmund, the pleasure resort of South West, on the Atlantic coast. The road is covered with salt residue, a cheap tar substitute where there is no rain

91. *below*, Swakopmund. Bounded by the sea and the dunes of the Namib

92. Salt mining near Swakopmund. Seawater is pumped into large flat
pans along the coast. When the water has evaporated the salt is scraped
from the surface

93. The Namib sand dunes form a desolate and almost impenetrable
barrier for hundreds of miles along the coast

94. A shipwreck on Skeleton coast. Many ships have been lost here;
any survivors from the wrecks have almost always perished in the quick-
sands or in the Namib desert

95. The leather rosette worn by this Ovahimba beauty signifies that she is married

96. Woman wearing an elaborate Ekori ceremonial headdress

97. Ovahimba children doing the Frog Dance

98. Ovahimba girl surprised

99. Ovahimba woman of the Kaokoveld. The leather rosette in her
hair shows her to be married

100. The Ovahimbas are proud, free, primitive and self-supporting.
They plant crops, breed cattle and hunt game—a culture that has
remained static for centuries

101. In the more arid southern part of South West Africa Karakul sheep thrive

102. *overleaf*, a lonely land